VICTORY

Ten Fundamental Beliefs that Eradicate Defeat in the Life of a Christian

Dr. John R. Adolph

Victory by Dr. John R. Adolph
Copyright © 2016 by John R. Adolph
All Rights Reserved.

ISBN: 978-1-59755-422-0

Published by: ADVANTAGE BOOKS™
Longwood, Florida, USA
www.advbookstore.com

This book and parts thereof may not be reproduced in any form, stored in a retrieval system or transmitted in any form by any means (electronic, mechanical, photocopy, recording or otherwise) without prior written permission of the author, except as provided by United States of America copyright law.

Scriptures quotation taken from The Holy Bible, King James Version, public domain.

Library of Congress Catalog Number: 2016957826

First Printing: December 2016
25 26 27 28 29 30 31   10 9 8 7 6 5 4 3 2

Victory

This Book is dedicated to:

- Our Resurrected Redeemer, Jesus Christ.
- Dorrie, Sumone, and Jonathan.
- Seymour and Barbara Adolph, Sr.
- Sonny, Nell, and Ron.
- Albertina and Vincent Washington.
- June Jones, Brooklyn Williams, Felicia Young.
- James Mable, Sheliah Moss, Jewel Cooper, Albert Moore, Diandra Darby, Cheryl Williams, Shatonna Hatch.
- Ronnie Leday, Robert Trahan, Malinda Pugh.
- Alexus Perry, Michelle Turner, Major Goldman III.
- Jack Gay, Katherine Briggs, Tonya Harris, Shelton Wiltz, Vickie Phillips, Lorraine Lemons, Porchanee White, Deacons, Trustees and The Antioch Church Family.

John R. Adolph

Table of Contents

Acknowledgements 7

Introduction... 9

  1: *Victory Through The Word* 11

  2: *Victory Through Prayer* 17

  3: *Victory Through The Holy Ghost* 25

  4: *Victory Through Faith In God* 31

  5: *Victory Through Grace And Salvation* 39

  6: *Victory Through Praise And Worship* 47

  7: *Victory Through The Cross Of Christ* 57

  8: *Victory In Spiritual Warfare* 69

  9: *Victory In The Kingdom Of God* 79

  10: *Victory Through The Second Coming Of Christ* ... 93

Conclusion 101

Other Books and Articles by John R. Adolph 103

John R. Adolph

Victory

Acknowledgements

When I consider the origins of this book my heart races in retrospect to a seminary class taught by Dr. John C. Diamond, professor of Philosophy at the Interdenominational Theological Center in Atlanta, Georgia. It was a five-hour lecture and there was never a boring moment. He stretched us biblically, pressed us intellectually and pushed us academically. I loved it.

On one occasion, he was asked a probing soteriological question while standing at the board filling it with notes, as he often did during each class time. A young lady from New Jersey lifted her hand and said piercingly, "Dr. Diamond, are you saved?" He paused and stared for a moment. He then turned slowly towards the class and replied, "If you are asking me if I have been baptized, if I have recited your creedal statements before a group of church folks or if I have been filled with the Holy Ghost my answer to you is that's none of your business. But, since you had the nerve to ask me, let me tell you this, my God is too big just to get to know in a day. It has been a journey and each day with God gets sweeter and sweeter. I am not just saved by your standards; I am a victory based on the essence of the reality of my God."

Did you hear that? I am a victory! I will never forget those words as long as I live. I had never heard it put on this order before. Here they are again just in case you missed them the first time; I am a victory! It is here that we find the core, crux, and center of this work. When you look into a mirror what do you see? The shocking reality is this, what you see is what you will soon be! My prayer for you, as you embark upon this study of faith fundamentals given in this book, is that when you see yourself from now on, you will see what God created:

The Salt of the Earth
The Light of the World
A Disciple
An Heir of God
A Joint Heir with Christ
An Overcomer
An Ambassador
 A Saint
A Soldier
A Son
A Child of God

VICTORY!!!

Victory

Introduction

The term victory appears in the Bible (KJV) eleven times and in the RSV some forty-four times. Each time that it is mentioned it is something that comes from God to you and not something that you do for yourself. Of course, you still have to fight, but you do not gain victory because you are so skillful in battle. You are graced with the victory because God has given it to you. Are you rejoicing yet? You should be and here is why, victory is yours!

Victory for the believer in Jesus Christ comes because we are in Him and He is in us. Apart from the Lord of Calvary, we are defeated on every hand, but with Him, we cannot lose. In fact, our victory in Christ is so intense, that even when we lose we still win! In short, there is no way to lose in Christ because Christ Jesus is the victory in you!

Knowing God comes with interconnectedness in knowing His Word and the truth that comes in it. This is why a book like this is so necessary. What you know impacts what you believe; what you believe shapes how you behave; and how you behave produces victory each day that you live. Therefore, the purpose of this book is to present Biblical truth that will shape what you believe and deliver victory for those that will trust God for it.

This work will cover ten faith fundamentals that will prove to both enlighten and empower you. Most importantly, I pray that they will lead you to the heart of God who will grant you victory in every possible way.

As you embark upon this study, let this truth settle in your heart and remain with you until you meet God face to face. You are not just victorious in Christ; you are a victory because of Christ! In fact, that is your new label. The word that describes your life in Jesus best is the word VICTORY!

Chapter 1

VICTORY
through the
WORD

Think About This

Victory starts the moment you pick up a Bible and believe what is in it. The moment you believe in Jesus Christ as both Lord and Savior, the moment you believe the God of heaven has a perfect plan for your life, the moment you believe God never leaves you nor forsakes you and the moment you know the book that is called the Bible is not just some ordinary book, your victory commences and never concludes.

Here is how it works. God is a God of revelation. He reveals to humanity His excellent works in many different ways. When the sun peeks over the eastern horizon to mark the genesis of a brand new day, it is God saying, "Consider the work of my hands." When stars shine brightly against the dark canvas of a midnight sky, it is the Lord of heaven saying, "Look at what I have done."

More importantly, God reveals Himself to us through the person of Jesus Christ. That's right; Jesus is God in a human body. Here is how John put it, ***"And the Word became flesh, and dwelt among us…" (John 1:14, KJV).*** Jesus said of Himself, ***"…he that hath seen me, hath seen the Father…" (John 14;9b, KJV).*** And, Paul puts it on this wise to the church at Colossae, ***"For in Him (Jesus Christ) dwelleth all the fullness of the Godhead bodily" (Col. 2:9).*** Get this, when Jesus walked the earth it was God in a human body saying to a dying world, "I love you."

Not only does God reveal Himself to us through creation, and through Christ, but through His Word. Therefore, the Bible is God's Word. It is the guide to your victory in both time and eternity.

Let's Go Deeper

The word Bible comes from the word *Biblia*, which means books. The Bible was later called "The Books" by some of the early church fathers like Clement. The term "Holy" translates as righteous or good and thus the Bible became known over time as the Holy Bible or the Good Book.

The Bible is God's inspired and inerrant revelation of the beginning and destiny of all things. The Bible says of itself,

1: VICTORY through the WORD

"All scripture is given by the inspiration of God…" (2 Tim. 3:16a). The term inspire in the Greek is *theopneustos*, and it means to breathe on something. So God breathed on men and guided them in their writing. With this in mind, the scriptures were given to us piecemeal. By this I mean, it was given to us a little bit at time. Holy men of God wrote as the Holy Spirit moved them during a period of about 1600 years, extending from about 1492 BC to nearly AD 100. God inspired kings like David and Solomon, political leaders like Daniel and Nehemiah, priests like Ezra, and men learned in the knowledge of Egypt like Moses. Men learned in Jewish law like Paul, by herdsmen like Amos, a tax collector like Matthew and a doctor like Luke were all responsible for inspirationally penning the pages of the Bible. God even used ignorant men like Peter, James, and John who were fisherman to give us His Word.

The Bible reveals to us God's plan and purpose for the ages. Christ is its grand subject, human good its design and the glory of Almighty God its ultimate end. It is the only book in the world that gives to the reader a record of the divine-human encounter, wherein a Holy and Righteous God interacts with sinful, fallen, hypocritical humankind. Therefore, the Bible presents to the reader the mind of God, the state of humanity, the way of salvation, the doom of the unsaved and the eternal happiness of those who believe. It contains light to direct you, food to sustain you and comfort to cheer you. Read it to be wise, trust it to be safe and practice it to be holy.

Here are some solid facts that a growing believer should know about the book that contains fundamental truth regarding spiritual victory.

THE BIBLE CONSISTS OF:

66 Books
2 Testaments-The Old Testament and the New Testament
39 Books in the Old Testament
27 Books in the New Testament

In the Old Testament, there are: 5 Books of the Law, 12 Books of Jewish History, 5 Books of Poetry, 5 Major Prophets, 12 Minor Prophets

In the New Testament, there are: 4 Gospels, 1 History Book, 14 Pauline Epistles, 7 General Epistles and 1 Book of Prophecy

The Bible Speaks 3 Cultural Languages: Hebrew, Aramaic, and Common Greek

1: VICTORY through the WORD

The Bible Speaks 3 Literary Languages: Figurative, Symbolic, and Literal

1,189 Chapters
31,102 Verses
783,137 Words
3,566,480 Letters
1,260 Promises
6,468 Commands
3,268 Verses of Fulfilled Prophecy
3,140 Verses of Unfulfilled Prophecy

Victory Happens Here

The book in your hand is the most compelling book the world has ever encountered. Jeremiah describes it as a "devouring flame" (Jer. 5:14) and "a crushing hammer" (Jer. 29:19). Ezekiel declares that it is a life-giving force (Eze. 37:1-7). Paul says it has saving power (Rom. 1:16) and an offensive weapon (Eph. 6:17). The writer of Hebrews calls it a "two-edged sword" (Heb. 4:12). There is nothing in the world like it! It heals, restores, directs, protects, keeps, comforts, saves, soothes, satisfies, rectifies and redeems! It is the road map to victory for all who believe.

John R. Adolph

Chapter 2

VICTORY
through
PRAYER

Think About This

Imagine for a moment that you were given the opportunity to crawl up into the lap of a ubiquitous, sovereign, omnipotent God and have a talk with Him and He with you. Imagine for a moment having a conversation with the creator of the universe. Think about what it would be like for you to have a chat with the one who gave you vocal chords and watched over you as you slumbered and slept. Imagine a talk with God. What would you say? How would you approach Him? What would you expect of Him? What do you think He would expect of you?

It is called prayer. As soon as you start to pray hell goes into a mode of panic because there is power in prayer. Prayer is a transcendent discipline, so you cannot see what happens when you start to pray. However, if you could see what takes place the moment you start to commune with the Lord of heaven in prayer, you would pray all of the time. Think about this, from the moment you say, "Heavenly Father..." the throne room of eternal glory tilts in your direction. God leans your way because He has been anticipating this moment and knew before you did that you would be calling Him. Angels that are near the Almighty come to attention because He just might decide to dispatch one to your charge. Demons become uncomfortable and Satan is reminded of the fact that he is a defeated foe. The bright countenance of the glory of God starts to radiate the darkness of the world around you as God says to your spirit, "Speak my child, your Father is listening."

Prayer is where the battle happens and prayer is the permanent place of your victory!

Let's Go Deeper

Prayer happens when you make contact, communicate and commune with the Christ of creation. It differs from praise and worship, in that praise is the occupation of the soul with its blessings; worship is the occupation of the soul with who God is and prayer is the occupation of the soul with its needs. Therefore, many times when you pray all three things take place.

2: Victory through Prayer

There are three fundamental types of prayer expressed throughout the scriptures and each one of them is incredibly powerful. First of all, there is requesting. This happens when you make a list and give it to God. Like a child taking its needs to a loving, caring parent, so you take your needs to the Lord. Secondly, there is intercession. It means to bear the burden of another. Intercession happens when you start to pray to God for the needs of someone else, instead of praying to God for you. Lastly, there is rejoicing. To rejoice is the most powerful form of prayer ever. It is where you spend your moments before God thanking Him for His goodness, grace, mercy, protection, provision, peace, and promises.

With this in mind, Jesus Christ taught His disciples to pray. He gave them what many of us call the Lord's Prayer as recorded in Matthew 6:9-13 which is a prayer outline. What the Lord was teaching His followers is this, when you pray here is how you should approach the Father, say this, ***"Our Father, which art in heaven hallowed be thy name. Thy Kingdom come, thy will be done in earth, as it is in heaven. Give us this day our daily bread. And forgive us our debts, as we forgive our debtors. And lead us not into temptation, but deliver us from evil. For thine is the Kingdom, and the power and the glory forever. Amen."***

Prayer to God should come from the soul and should consist of things like:

ADORATION: When you begin to pray start by giving God the glory for who He is and what He is to you. During this segment of prayer make it a point not to ask God for anything at all. Simply lift Him as your King, your Master, your Savior, your Doctor, your Provider and your Father. In short, adore, appreciate, applaud, and celebrate Him. Tell Him how much you love Him and how much you sincerely seek to please Him.

THANKSGIVING: During this segment of prayer, take the time to thank God for all of the many blessings He has already bestowed upon you. For the salvation that He has provided through the cross, for the precious person of the Holy Ghost, for the truth and treasure of His Word, for His grace, mercy, love, care, compassion, forgiveness, hope, help, healing and benefits, tell Him thank you.

SUPPLICATION: This is actually where you begin to make a specific list of things you need and give them to God. It is here you should make your requests known unto the Lord. Keep this in mind, as you go forth in this section of prayer, Jesus said, ***"Ask and it shall be given you, seek and ye shall find, knock and the door shall be opened unto you" (Matt. 7:7 KJV).***

THANKSGIVING: Yes more thanksgiving! This moment of thanksgiving is different from the first offering because you should now, in faith, thank God for what He is about to do.

2: Victory through Prayer

This takes a great deal of faith and trust in the Lord. This is where you say thank you for healing while the tumor is still inoperable. This is where you say thank you Jesus for the increase while you are still financially destroyed. This is where you say thank you Lord for the breakthrough while you are still going through.

THE NAME OF JESUS: Seal the prayer with His name. There is a reason why we conclude all petitions with our Savior's name. His name, and His name alone, represents the authority, ability, and the abundance of God. His name is above every name (Phil. 2:9).

Often when believers pray and their prayers are not answered immediately we give up and stop praying. However, that is not the time to stop but the time to pray like never before! Please remember this, to be delayed does not mean that you have been denied. In fact, there are times spiritual warfare is taking place between angels and demons that are invisible to the naked eye that is causing the delay. According to Daniel 10:1-15, Daniel had been praying for some twenty-one days before an angel brought him an answer. When the angel with the answer finally appeared, he informed Daniel that God had heard him the very first day. Because of demons at the river, he was delayed and needed assistance from the Archangel Michael to get the answer for the prayer.

When it seems like your prayers will not be answered, pray on! When it feels like God is on a deserted island wearing earplugs, pray on! When it seems like all hope is futile and you have been beset with serious issues, here is the best resolve ever, pray on!

With this in mind, there are times when God's answer to your request is no. No matter how much you pray, nothing will change Him until you make some changes. In short, there are some things that hinder our prayers to God. Here is a brief list of the things that can cause prayers to be hindered:

Instability and Doubt (James 1:6-8)
Disobedience (1 Samuel 14:37)
Marital Relations (1 Peter 3:7)
Unconfessed Sin (Psalms 66:18)
Lack of Humility (2 Chron. 7:14)
Selfish Prayers (James 4:3)
Refusal to Hear God's Word (Proverbs 28:9)
Worry and Anxiety (Phil. 4:6-7)
Neglect of Mercy (Proverbs 21:13)
Stubbornness (Zech. 7:12-13)

Just like some things can hinder our prayers, some things can empower prayer. One of those things, certainly worth mentioning, is fasting. Keep this in mind; prayer is a spiritual

2: Victory through Prayer

activity that does not appease the flesh. With this being said, there are times when fasting (abstaining from particular flesh appealing activity) can prove to be very powerful. Fasting keeps the flesh in subjection while you feed your spirit glorious communion with Almighty God.

Prayer is great, but fasting and praying takes prayer to another level. Fasting deepens what you receive in prayer. Imagine for a moment you were at the edge of the ocean. God, in this example, would be the deep blue sea and you would be the swimmer. Most believers only snorkel once or twice a week. They get a chance to see the beautiful creation that lies just beneath the surface. Now imagine removing your snorkel gear and going scuba diving. You would encounter another world. You would see things that the people who snorkel just cannot see. They are just not deep enough. Fasting is to prayer what scuba diving is to the sea! It takes your encounter with the sea to another level.

In the bible, the church leaders at Antioch did it (Acts 13:2-3) and Jesus recommended it to His disciples if they wanted to see miracles take place (Matt. 17:21). Real ministry starts with a fast (Matt. 4:1-9) and fasting empowers and purifies the body of a believer for greater service to God (Joel 1:14).

Victory Happens Here

Never forget this, your prayers are so filled with victory that God keeps every one and stores them in a vial in heaven. They are stored under the altar and when God wants to fill heaven with a beautiful fragrance, He calls for an angel to bring Him the prayers of the saints. That angel opens the vial and your prayers fill heaven with a sweet aroma (Rev. 5:8, Rev. 8:3)!

Chapter 3

VICTORY
through the
HOLY GHOST

Think About This

He walks with you. He talks with you. He teaches you. He guides you. He seals you. He protects you. He lifts you. He heals you. He saves you. He strengthens you. He blesses you. He loves you. He guards you. He governs you. He escorts you. He befriends you. He speaks to you. He inspires you. He empowers you. He energizes you. He enlightens you. He engulfs you. He fills you. He refills you. He sustains you. He ignites you. He prepares you. He uses you. He holds you. He molds you. He soothes you. He propels you. He calls you. He interrupts you. He elevates you. He emancipates you. He liberates you. He situates you. He created you. He formed you. He fashioned you. He made you!

Who is He you ask? He is the source of your victory. He is the reason you win! He is the sweetest person in the whole wide world. He is God in the Spirit. The Bible calls Him THE HOLY GHOST.

Let's Go Deeper

The Holy Ghost is not an it! He is the third person of the Godhead that makes up the trinity. He is coequal, coexistent and coeternal with God the Father and God the Son. He is God the Holy Ghost. In the Old Testament, the Holy Spirit did not function as He did in the New Testament or for that matter during our present day. In the Old Testament, He rested upon men and empowered them to do great and mighty works for God. However, in the New Testament until our present day, the Holy Spirit does not rest upon those who believe, He dwells within those who believe (St. John 14:17, Romans 8:9, 1 Cor. 3:16, and 1 John 2:27).

Did you just rejoice over this truth? You should have and here is why. The same God that called Abraham to follow Him lives in you. The same God that was with Moses at the Red Sea lives in you. The same God that met the woman of Samaria at the well lives in you.

The Holy Spirit was given to believers on earth for several reasons. All of these divinely inspired realities are given

3: VICTORY through the HOLY GHOST

explicitly in scripture. Let's explore a few of these fantastic concepts.

First of all, the Holy Spirit was given to all believers to empower the church's witness. The church started with just one hundred and twenty people. They were an ordinary, salt of the earth people. In Acts 1:8, Luke tells us that the Holy Spirit was given to the early church so that they might be witnesses for Jesus Christ in Jerusalem (the city), Judea (the country), Samaria (foreign lands) and in the uttermost parts of the world (land not yet discovered).

This is what took place on the day of Pentecost recorded in Acts 2. Jesus knew the one hundred and twenty who gathered in Jerusalem believed in the resurrection. However, He knew it would take Holy Ghost power to cause them to witness while facing persecution. Therefore, He gave them Him in the form of the Holy Ghost.

Secondly, the Holy Spirit was given to us to impart life. This is to say, that the Spirit of God who dwells in us gives us life and life everlasting. Paul put it this way, ***"But if the Spirit of Him that raised up Jesus from the dead dwell in you, He that raised up Christ from the dead shall also quicken your mortal bodies by His Spirit that dwelleth in you" (Rom. 8:11, KJV)***. In short, anything without the Spirit is dead and anything with the Spirit is alive.

Thirdly, the Holy Spirit teaches us. Consider this, Noah built the Ark, but he was not an engineer and had no boat building experience (Gen. 6-9). How did he do it? Here is the answer, the Holy Spirit taught him. Moses was able to make the bitter waters of Morah sweet with the use of a stick from a tree (Exodus 15:22-26). Moses was not a marine engineer. He was raised in Egypt and was a shepherd for his father-in-law. How did he do it? Here is the truth, the Holy Spirit taught him. Peter had no medical experience whatsoever. In fact, he was a fisherman by trade. He healed a lame man at the gate called Beautiful (Acts 3). How did he do it? You've got it, the Holy Spirit taught him.

The Holy Spirit is the greatest teacher the world has never laid an eye on. He is invisible, but He is audible. You cannot see Him, but He can be heard. There are times He can be heard in the still small silence of the soul. Other times He can be heard through the voice of your Pastor, a teacher of scripture or some other vessel of His choosing. Whatever the case, when He speaks you cannot miss it.

Please hold on to this truth, there are times that we as believers can sense the Holy Spirit directing us to do one thing and we do something entirely different. It is where we quench the Spirit (1 Thess. 5:19). This happens when we disobey or even ignore the sweet voice of God seeking to give us direction. Defeat often comes to those who ignore Him; victory always comes to those who obey Him.

Lastly, the Holy Spirit guides every aspect of our lives. He helps us pray (Rom. 8:26). He helps us see (John 14:17). He empowers us to choose right when wrong is staring us in the face (John 16:13). John the Apostle says it like this, ***"But ye have an unction from the Holy One and ye know all things" (1 John 2:20, KJV).*** With this in mind, He guides, guards and governs all believers.

When you confess belief in Jesus Christ, two things happens at once that give you victory in God for the rest of your life. First of all, you are sealed with the Holy Ghost. You are stamped and it is never removed. You belong to God and that is that. Read Ephesians 1:13-14. This seal lasts forever. It happens once and for all.

Secondly, you are filled with the Holy Ghost. He is a gift given to every believer at the moment of saving faith in Jesus Christ. Read John 7:37-39. The filling of the Spirit differs from the sealing of the Spirit, in that you are sealed forever. However, you need to be filled and refilled over and over again throughout the course of your life (Eph. 5:18).

Victory Happens Here

Here is your shout of victory regarding the person of the Holy Spirit: He has you covered from the inside out! This is why you cannot lose. On the outside, He seals you and on the inside He fills you. No matter what, you are in Him and He is in you. As long as you have Him and He has you, victory is always yours and here is why:

He Is The Author of All Scripture (2 Tim. 3:16)
He Is Your Comforter and Escort (John 14:16)
He Convicts You Of What Is Wrong (John 16:7-11)
He Guides You Into What Is Right (John 16:13)
He Is Your Seal & Deposit (Eph. 1:13-14)
He Is Your Intercessor (Romans 8:26)
He Is Your Revealer (John 14:17)
He Is Your Teacher (John 14:26)
He Is Your Life and Victory (Rom. 8:2)

Chapter 4

VICTORY through *FAITH IN GOD*

Think About This

It believes the unbelievable. It can see the invisible. It can move the unmovable. It can pass the unsurpassable. It can hold onto something when nothing exists. It can say thank you before the need is met. It can shout about victory while looking at defeat. It can thank God for a resurrection while sitting at the funeral of a loved one. It can celebrate the promise of God before the promise comes to pass. It can help you endure hell on earth while you press your way towards heaven that will come later. It can make you sow a tithe, which is a dime, knowing that you will reap a harvest, which will manifest itself as dollars. It can hope when all hope is gone. It is the root of every miracle. It is the fruit of every soul that is saved and baptized. It is what has brought us this far and it is what will carry us on.

What is it? Don't you want to know? Here it is and do not forget it; it is FAITH.

Faith and defeat cannot coexist. If you are defeated, it is because the light of your faith has been blown out by the turbulent winds of doubt in your life. But if you have faith and confidence in the person of Jesus Christ you have victory and cannot see defeat.

Let's Go Deeper

Faith is the modus operandi of the believer. It is our mode of operation. Everything under the sun has a mode of operation. For a car, it is the engine. For television, it is the video screen. For a computer, it is the drive. For a shovel, it is the blade. With this in mind, faith is how a believer functions. It is what God expects of us. We operate not by what we see, not by what we think, not logic, reason or statistical data. We are victorious people of faith!

We walk by faith (2 Cor. 5:7). We live by faith (Heb. 10:38). We are saved through faith (Eph. 2:8). We are healed by faith (Mark 2:5). Faith does everything that we do or it is not done at all. With this in mind, the word faith appears two hundred and twenty-four times in the Bible (KJV). It is mentioned only twice in the Old Testament (Deut. 32:20 and

4: VICTORY through FAITH IN GOD

Hab. 2:4) and in each instance, it means firm or secure in one's convictions.

In the New Testament, the word is mentioned two hundred and twenty-two times. In most cases, it translates from the Greek word *pistis*. It means to trust completely, to rest upon or to be entirely convinced. This is why the writer of Hebrews argues it like this, ***"Now faith is the substance of things hoped for, the evidence of things not seen" (Heb.11:1).*** It is also why Paul Tillich taught, "Faith was our ultimate concern." It is why Dr. E. K. Bailey preached with a passion that "faith is acting like a thing is so, even when it is not so, so that it might be so."

Here is an important note to remember, never confuse faith and belief as many do. Faith is a component of belief. This is why Jesus never called His Disciples "beliefless." He always called them "faithless." This is because you cannot have faith in something that you do not believe in. Belief is triune. It consists of faith (the action on what is believed), trust (places reliance on faith's action) and hope (reaches forth in anticipation to what is believed).

With this in mind, many people see the church as a group of believers who need more faith. However, this is not the case; the church is often filled with faithless religious people who are unbelievers. This is why we do not see God move in our midst in many instances. We have religion but no faith.

But, when we have faith in God and take Him at His Word, healing and deliverance takes place like never before.

Please know that there is only one way to get faith. The Bible says it clearly, ***"So then faith cometh by hearing and hearing by the Word of God" (Rom. 10:17).*** Notice if you will, that real faith is not taught, it is caught. It is just like the lyrics to your favorite song. You learned them because you kept hearing them. When you heard them enough, you started singing them yourself. You did not take a class. You heard the words until you caught them. So it is with faith, you need to hear God's Word until it becomes a part of who you are. Hear it until you catch it!

Here is one huge problem that many of us have. We listen and do not hear. That is right; we confuse hearing and listening all of the time. Hearing demands a response and listening only means to perceive sound with the ear. Therefore, you can listen and never understand a word that has been spoken. For example, imagine walking into a church in Spain. The cathedral would be beautiful. The stained glass windows would be breathtaking. The preacher mounted the pulpit and gave a stirring message; to which numerous people gave their lives to Christ. You were excited to see it all take place. But, if you do not speak Spanish, you could listen attentively, but you would not understand a word that the preacher said.

4: VICTORY through FAITH IN GOD

Jesus Christ often said, ***"He that hath ears to hear, let him hear" (Matt. 13:9, 13:43, 21:33).*** Why? The reason is simple, everybody with ears cannot hear.

The most important facet of faith is how faith works. Faith is subjective and needs an object to declare what it is worth. In other words, it is what we have faith in that determines what our faith is possible of doing. Keep this in mind; you cannot expect any more from your faith than what the object of your faith is capable of producing.

For example, let's assume that the object of our faith is money. If we have faith in money, we can safely say that there are a lot of things that money (the object of our faith) can buy. However, since this is true, we cannot expect money to meet our every need because there are a lot of things that money just cannot buy. In other words, money, the object of our faith is limited, so our faith is limited.

Imagine for a moment that you have a best friend who is an airplane pilot and he has the best safety record in the world. He invites you to fly to Nassau for three days of fun and relaxation. Without delay, you accept his generous offer. You call your job to get the days off, pack your bags and leave for the airport. When you reach the airport and prepare to board the aircraft, you discover that the airplane that your friend has is not an MD747. Instead, it is his latest invention. The plane is made out of plywood, two old car seats and a lawnmower engine. You look at the aircraft in disgust. Your trip has been ruined. Your friend smiles and boasts on his safety record. But you tell him that you do not want to travel with him because his plane is no good. Then your friend turns to you and says, "Where is your faith?"

You see, it is not that you do not have faith. But you can clearly see that the object of your faith, the airplane, has extremely limited possibilities.

Can I give you an early victory shout right quick? The object of your faith as a believer in Jesus Christ is God! Your faith in God can do what God does. This is what provoked Paul to say, *"I can do all things through Christ which strengthens me" (Phil. 4:13).* It is also why Jesus taught His disciples, *"….if ye have the faith as a grain of mustard seed, ye shall say unto this mountain, remove, and nothing shall be impossible unto you" (Matt. 17:20b, KJV).* Faith in God does the impossible because the God of your faith can accomplish the incredible! Your faith in Him can do what He is capable of doing.

Victory Happens Here

The Bible is clear; every believer has been given the measure of faith (Rom. 12:3). With this in mind, activate your faith right now and victory will be the result. Here is how you activate your faith:

4: VICTORY through FAITH IN GOD

SAY IT (Proverbs 18:21)
DO IT (James 2:17-18)
RECEIVE IT (Acts 3:1-8)
TELL IT (Rev. 12:11)

John R. Adolph

Chapter 5

VICTORY
through
GRACE AND SALVATION

Think About This

Religion is the world's greatest mistake. It is the path to defeat and millions travel this road every single day. Religion is best defined as humankind seeking God's approbation based solely on good works. Systems of religion the world over demand that you pray so many times a day, that you refrain from certain activity, that you work for the right of satisfying God based on things that you do. So in the name of religion, people do all types of things. For instance, Muslims refuse to eat pork and Hindus do not eat any form of meat for fear that they could be partaking of a loved one who has returned in reincarnation as an animal and the list goes on and on.

The blessing of being a Christian is that our victory does not come to us in the form of religion with a comprehensive list of things that you can and cannot do attached. It is a relationship with God Himself, through Jesus Christ, His only begotten Son. Our system of belief does not give us a list of rules to follow. It grants us a parental relationship with God that allows us to call Him Father, Daddy, and even Big Daddy. As a Christian, we are adopted into the family of God with legal rights to call Jesus Christ our Elder Brother and the Holy Spirit our eternal friend. With this in mind, we do not get a list of rules to follow, which if we fail or falter in trying to keep them, we get kicked out of the club. That is not how salvation works. We have a relationship with a loving Father who has very high standards for His children. When we miss a standard or make a mess of things, He picks us up, wipes the dust off our past mistakes and empowers us to continue onward until we meet the standards that He has set for us (John 15:1-6). Does this sound like a religion to you?

Wait there is more. Not only are you in the family of God, but also you are included in the will of the wealthiest source that has and will ever exist. You are in the will of God, marked as one of His Children and can claim with legal rights a part of the royal inheritance.

Okay, wait, one more thing and this should bring tears to your eyes. God made a decision in eternity past to choose you.

5: VICTORY through GRACE AND SALVATION

He wanted you in His family and knew about your flaws, failures, mishaps, missteps, misfortunes and still wanted you.

Does this sound like a religion to you? It is not. It is a relationship offered by God to all of humankind that comes to us through salvation by grace alone, through faith alone, through Christ alone! It is not based on your human effort; it has nothing to do with how many worship services you attend on a regular basis or how many nice things you do for other people. Our relationship has everything to do with God's eternal gift to you in the person of Jesus Christ. This my friend spells victory!

Let's Go Deeper

Salvation for the Christian comes through something the Bible calls grace (Eph. 2:8). The word grace should make the soul of any real Christian smile. Grace is God's unmerited favor towards you. It is God giving you what you cannot buy, cannot charge and cannot afford. It is God doing for you that which you cannot do for yourself. It is the kindness of God expressed towards you whether you deserve it or not. It is His richest blessing poured out upon a world filled with sinners.

The Bible clearly reveals four realms of God's grace. There is Provisional Grace. This realm of grace provides everything that we need as human beings to live on free of charge. Provisional grace provides rain for the just and the unjust. It provides sunlight for the good and the bad. It furnishes air to breathe for the guilty and the innocent. It supplies a gentle breeze for both the sinner and the saint. It is this grace that affirms the fact that God is Jehovah Jireh (Gen. 22:14). He still provides.

Not only is there provisional grace, but also there is Sustaining Grace. The Lord's sustaining grace keeps those things He provides for us from running out. So the sun never runs out of sunshine, the moon never stops glowing, stars never stop shinning, the rain falls at just the right time. Sustaining grace keeps the earth on its axis and keeps it turning at just the right speed. If we were to move too fast, we would freeze to death and if we were to move too slow, we would burst into flames. Sustaining grace makes sure that winter is cold enough to produce an enchanting spring and summer is hot enough to produce a beautiful fall (Heb. 1:3).

The third realm of grace is called Salvitic Grace. This form of grace is what makes God's grace so amazing. Here is how it works. In eternity past, God carefully constructed a redemptive plan that would save sinners and produce saints. This plan brings us to the courtroom of eternal justice, where God is the Judge (Is. 33:22, James 4:12), the adversary and accuser of the brethren is Satan (Rev. 12:10) and you are on trial for sins you have committed and have been found guilty as charged (Rom. 6:23). You stand and declare to the

5: VICTORY through GRACE AND SALVATION

righteous Judge that you are guilty and He sentences you to death. It is what you deserve for the sins you have committed.

All hope seems lost, right? This is where the redemptive plot thickens and amazing grace shows it beautiful face. God knew that you would meet Him and deserve death, so He fixed it! He gave us His only begotten Son, Jesus Christ, to be the perfect ransom for the error of your ways (1 Tim. 2:6). That is right; God loves you so much that He peeled off divinity, wrapped Himself in humanity and came to earth just to redeem you (Phil. 2:5-11, St. John 3:16, Eph. 1:7)! Are you shouting yet? You should be and here is why; He paid a debt that He did not owe because you owed a debt to the court of law that you could not pay. Now here is what is so profound, the payment for sin required a sacrifice, so Jesus had to die. Howbeit, He died a substitutionary death. Jesus died in your place. He remained in the grave for three days, but early the third day morning, He rose from the grave with all power in His hands (2 Cor. 5:21, 1 Cor. 15:3, Rom. 5:6, Rom. 5:8, St. Matt. 28:18). Now that Jesus has died and risen, salvation by grace alone, through faith alone in the person of Jesus Christ alone is in full effect.

Let's go back to the courtroom. You are still standing before the Judge and He has condemned you to death. The doors of the courtroom open and your attorney walks in. He is the lawyer with the holes still in His hands left from His suffering at the cross. He whispers to you and says, "We have this case beat. Be quiet, let me do all of the talking." He then speaks as your advocate and legal counsel. He asks the Judge for permission to approach the bench. The sovereign Judge honors His request to be heard. It is then that your lawyer says, "Your honor the debt for all of the crimes that my client owed this court has been paid for in full. I personally sacrificed it all for my client so that they might go free." While Satan watches, the righteous Judge will declare you are innocent and justified of all charges. The righteous Judge will then state as a matter of legal record; this case has been dismissed!

Now here is the shout of a lifetime, when the court proceedings are concluded you discover that the Judge was your attorney's Father and they have decided to adopt you into their family. When you leave the courtroom that day, you leave not only being declared innocent, even though you are guilty, but you have the legal right to call the Judge Daddy!

Victory Happens Here

The last realm of grace is called Life Changing Grace. It is the grace the Lord gives to His children while we are being molded into the image of His Son because we all still sin and miss the mark that is set before us. The reason why God does

5: VICTORY through GRACE AND SALVATION

not throw us away or give up on us is that He has decided to give every believer "more grace" (James 4:6).

Does this sound like a religion to you? Salvation by grace alone demands some gratitude from those in the family of God. In fact, here is your chance for a moment of victory rejoicing, grace comes from the Greek word *charis* and it is a reference to God's undeserved goodness bestowed upon you. The Latin root of the word grace is *gratia.* We borrow the word gratitude from it. Now here is where your victory shout goes, for all of the grace that you have received you should always have some gratitude for a Father like yours who graces you with victory in the face of defeat!

John R. Adolph

Chapter 6

VICTORY
through
PRAISE AND WORSHIP

Think About This

It is loud, boisterous, attention getting and quite disturbing at times. Cowboy fans do it when the men wearing the star score a touchdown. It happens in New York City when the men on the diamond, they call Yankees, win another championship. It even occurs in the city of Cleveland, Ohio when the Cavaliers find themselves in the winner's circle again after being absent for nearly half a century. Do you know what it is?

Wait before you answer. We can find it on Bourbon Street in the crescent city of New Orleans during the celebration of Mardi Gras. It happens every night in Las Vegas at casinos when people finally have a slot machine that pays big time. It even takes place when you are in the tiny town of Baldwin,

Louisiana when a scratch off lotto playing sister finally wins the pick six. Do you know what it is yet?

Hold on, before you answer. Consider this, it is encountered on college campuses during the month of March for what they call March Madness. It even happens at area high schools in the fall of the year when the kids wearing pads and shiny helmets hit the field. You even hear it coming from the nightclub when the music is loud, the cups are empty and people with various spirits from the alcohol are moving to the beat of the music and the party is at its peak.

What is it you asked? It is praise and worship. The problem is that in every instance listed previously the God that we serve is neither the object nor the subject of it, which makes it nothing more than just a bunch of noise. However, when we decide to give the Lord of heaven and earth what He truly deserves, it should fill the land with a shout and a joyful noise that cannot be compared to anything the earth has ever felt, heard or seen.

This is what praise and worship are all about! It is about giving the God of glory the rightful glory He deserves. Most importantly, it is an outward, audible and impressionable sign that victory belongs to those who believe!

Let's Go Deeper

Let's set the record straight from the onset of this chapter; you were created to give God praise. The Bible says,

"Let them praise the name of the Lord, for He commanded, and they were created." (Psalms 148:5)

"Thou art worthy, O Lord, to receive glory and honor and power; for thou hast created all things and for thy pleasure they are and were created." (Rev. 4:11)

"Bless the Lord, O my soul: and all that is within me, bless His holy name." (Psalms 103:1)

"Let everything that hath breath praise the Lord. Praise ye the Lord." (Psalms 150:6)

Make no mistake about it, the God of heaven says, "I both desire and deserve your praise and your worship." Now here is what can be somewhat tricky. There are times that a prayer sounds like praise and there are moments when praise looks just like worship. Even though these Christian practices are very similar, they can be separated.

Remember this, prayer is the occupation of the soul with its needs. So when prayer takes place, there will usually be some form of petition or request we lay before God.

If prayer deals with human need and sacred petitions, then praise becomes the occupation of the soul with its blessings. With this in mind, praise is the gratitude we express to God for the wonderful things He has done for us. When God has been kind, merciful, compassionate and has done numerous life changing things for you, the proper response is to praise Him. It is worthy of note that anyone can praise God. Praise only requires gratitude and not conversion.

Worship is entirely different. Worship is the occupation of the soul with who God is. Worship then is to adore God, to know Him, to love Him, to seek to be near Him and most importantly to live for Him each and every day. Worship is a lifestyle. It is what you do in your body and is considered your reasonable service to God (Rom. 12:1). In fact, the word worship in the Greek is *proskeneo* and it means to kiss. Therefore, worship requires intimacy with the Lord. There must be a relationship present to worship God. One that says, "I am not just clapping and singing, but I am living to honor you every moment of the day."

Please understand this, the praise of God is not like items you pick up from a buffet. As a Christian, you do not have the luxury of praising God the way you want to. Praise is specific

6: VICTORY through PRAISE AND WORSHIP

and detailed. In other words, there are specified precepts, principles and practices set in scripture for the praise of the Lord. Here is a brief list for you to read, retain and rehearse:

Barak-Kneel before God

Kneeling before God is an outward sign of inward humility and reverence for who He is. (Psalms 34:1, 95:6)

Yadah-Lift the Hands Cupped

To lift the hands cupped to the Lord is a sign of total dependence. Like a child raises his hands to a parent, so it is that you raise your hands to the Lord. (Psalms134:2, 141:2)

Tehillah-Sing before the Lord

Singing to God does not require a beautiful voice. It does, however; require that your soul be saved, for only the redeemed have a song to sing. (Psalms 40:3, 149:1)

Shabach-To Shout

Shouting before the Lord is an outward display of adoration that says to the world our God is worthy and He alone is victorious. (Psalms 47:1)

Zamar-To Play Instruments

God is a music lover and He adores when music has Him in mind and heart. Please know, that there is no such thing as Christian music, there is only Christian lyrics. What makes music Christian is when a Christian honors the Lord with their skill and plays to honor Him in spirit and in true. (Psalms 33:2, 150)

Todah-To express gratitude and thankfulness to God

In acts of both praise and worship thank you to God is appropriate. This gratitude should have its roots in your heart and should be expressed with your soul to God. (Psalms 50:14, 69:30 and 100:4)

Halal-To shout without shame

There are times that human pride rears its ugly head and we become prideful and even embarrassed to adore God in praise. But when that moment comes seek to halal the Lord, shout without any shame. (Psalms 44:8, 63:5)

Kawrar-To Dance, to wheel around in a circular motion

Some people waltz, while others dance the tango. Still, there are some that zydeco and others that calypso. However, in the act of worship, we Kawrar the Lord. It is to wheel around in a simple circle. It is what David did when he danced before Lord. (Psalms 149:3, 150:4, 2 Sam. 6:14)

Hawsaw-To be silent before the Lord

Keep in mind that a quiet praise happens when you are about to see God do something great in your presence. Our elders used to hawsaw the Lord when it started to thunder and lightening. It was their way of saying, be silent while God shows us how great He is. (Ex. 14:13, Zach. 2:13, Rev. 8:1-3)

Taqa-Clapping the Hands

To clap the hands produces noise. A noise that says to anyone near, that you are alive and that your God is still in control. This is why Israel is told to clap and this is why we clap during praise and worship. (Psalms 47:1)

The Bible reminds us never to forsake the assembling of ourselves together (Heb. 10:25). One reason for this is because some forms of praise require more than one person to produce. All of the previous forms of praise can be done alone. You can sing by yourself, dance by yourself, shout by yourself and express thankfulness by yourself. But, some forms of praise require the presence of other believers to assist you in the process. Three forms of praise require a community of believers to produce. They are as follows:

Gawal-Magnify the Lord

The word magnify means to plait or twist. It means to braid. Here is how it works, like you would braid hair, believers come together to make large their praise for the Lord by twisting their gratitude together to make one huge praise before God. (Psalms 34:3, 69:30)

Kawbade-Glorify the Lord

This term means to make an object heavy or to make something numerous. As it relates to praising God, it means for you to gather together with other believers and stack your gratitude in one huge heavy pile. Imagine for a moment, everyone walking into a worship service carrying a brick. One brick is not that heavy and it is certainly not numerous. But, now consider everyone just stacking their bricks to make one huge heavy pile. This is how we glorify the Lord. We stack our gratitude and make our thanksgiving heavy for Him. (Psalms 34:3)

Room-Exalt the Lord

To exalt the Lord means to lift Him high. In a very practical sense, it means to build a pyramid of praise for Him. Have you ever seen cheerleaders build a pyramid? You know, they put the girls with hips on the bottom, with the smallest girls up top. This is done to cheer on a team, but the same thing happens in the spirit when we exalt the Lord. We gather together with other saints to build a pyramid of praise unto Him. To stack it as high as it can go because He alone is worthy of being praised. (Psalms 34:3)

Victory Happens Here

Have you noticed that all of this praise talk requires noise? Why so much noise? Why is all of this singing, clapping, shouting and dancing necessary? Please do not ever forget this, losers don't make noise! Dead people don't make noise! Your praising God with a joyful noise is both a sign and symbol. It is a symbol of your victory and it is a sign to the world that your God is still on the throne!

In fact, you should conclude this whole chapter by shouting alleluia! Get this, Alleluia is to give God the highest praise ever. It translates praise ye Jah. Jah is one of the Hebrew names for God, which means the self-existing one. Therefore, when you shout Alleluia, what you are saying is no one deserves the praise but God. He alone is worthy. This word is only found in the New Testament four times and all four times it is recorded in heaven and is used to celebrate heavens victory before the battle ever commences (Rev. 19:1, 19:3-4, 19:5)!

Your battle has been fought! Your victory has been won! The enemy has been defeated! You are victorious in Jesus Christ! Alleluia!

Chapter 7

VICTORY
through the
CROSS OF CHRIST

Think About This

When the word victory is mentioned what image comes to your mind? Maybe the face of a ferocious lion or perhaps even the image of a huge muscular man that seems invincible. Some would even envision the majestic flight of an eagle soaring high above a mountain. Victory, what does it look like to you?

It could look like a student that is celebrating commencement or an Olympic athlete on the bema receiving a gold medal for crossing the finish line in first place. It may even look like a woman ringing the bell after surviving a bout with breast cancer and now she can let the whole world know that she is cancer free.

When you hear someone say victory what image pops into your head? As a believer in Jesus Christ, victory takes on a geometric construct. It looks like a figure that would start on earth and reach high enough into the heavens to touch the heart of God while He is seated sovereignly on His throne. A figure tall enough to grip the grace of God and cause Him to shower all of humanity with new mercies every single morning. It would look like a figure that could reach low enough to touch the depths of hell with its redemptive love. It would have to be broad enough to fit the "whosoever will" into its cross beam. Can you see it? It is for us the emblem of suffering and shame. It is for us a figure that would have been used to perform an execution. Victory for the Christian is shaped like a cross!

All too often in our culture, we see a cross as nothing more than a cute brooch to accompany a nice outfit or even a tattoo on someone's arm or leg. But, please hear this, it is so much more. Eternal salvation comes from the cross. Justification, sanctification, propitiation, expiation and glorification are all found near the cross. Healing happens because of the cross. Peace with God occurs around the cross. Life is found in the cross and a resurrection indeed comes after the cross.

The cross! It is the place where sinners are brought to the bleeding side of an innocent sacrifice for the purpose of forgiveness, mercy, grace and another chance. The cross! The place where a lost world can find hope without price, freedom without fee and help without an invoice attached. The cross! The place where sinners become saints and where wayward fallen guilt-ridden people become the adopted children of God. The cross! The place where the redemptive shores of eternal glory touch the wretched boundaries of human real estate and bring victory and life to every dead situation and circumstance. The cross!

Make no mistake about it, victory for the child of God looks like a cross!

Let's Go Deeper

Every culture that has supported capital punishment since the time of the flood has come up with creative ways to do away with social undesirables. The Assyrians would starve a man until his body was weak and then bury him standing up in the sand. They would bury everything except for his head. They would leave him there until the scorching hot Mesopotamian sun caused his tongue to swell in his mouth and he would die by way of suffocation.

The Babylonians used the old fiery furnace and the Egyptians would take a man to the hottest part of the desert, stake him to the ground and let the sun beat him until his internal organs would swell. Death would be slow and painful. Jews used a method called stoning. They would throw a man off a cliff and then finish the job by throwing rocks at him until he was completely covered. In America, we are much more civilized and dignified. We use lethal injection to put a man to death.

Throughout the course of human history, capital punishment has been used, but no one was as good at it as the Romans. In fact, Rome created ways to torture, dehumanize and destroy persons they thought deserved such punishment. There were times that Caesar would have a man thrown to horrible man-eating beasts in a coliseum and allowed thousands of spectators to watch as he was devoured in public. If that weren't good enough, he would tie a person's body to a huge post, pour flammable liquid on him, set his body ablaze and use the burning corpse to light up a banquet hall. Moreover, if that was not the method used, the Romans were known for scourging. To be scourged means that they would skin you while you were alive. This was done by taking a large leather whip that was filled with lead and sharp pieces of bone at the tip. The whip was then used to beat a man publicly for crimes he committed. Lashes from this whip were known to leave a man near dead or kill him.

When the Roman government wanted to do the job right, they used a method called crucifixion. This was the worst form of capital punishment ever. It was designed to punish a person severely and eventually death would come by

7: VICTORY through the CROSS OF CHRIST

suffocation, after being nailed to a tree alive. To make matters worse, the Romans would make a public display of the social undesirables. They would let their naked bodies hang on the cross until they could no longer push their bodies up high enough to inhale or exhale. When they could no longer breathe, they died. Can you imagine someone enduring this kind of torture for you? This is what Jesus Christ did for you and He did it so that you might have victory in every aspect of your life.

Now here is the real question that beckons us to grapple with it. Why? Why would Jesus Christ endure this kind of suffering for us? Was the cross necessary? The resounding answer is yes!

The cross was necessary because it was a fulfillment of prophecy foreshadowed. In Exodus 12, the children of Israel are in Egyptian bondage and captivity. God has summoned His servant Moses to return with his brother

Aaron to inform Pharaoh that he must let Israel go. God hardened Pharaoh's heart and the Lord of heaven put in place a feast called the Passover. This feast was to take place with a male lamb, without blemish. The lamb was to be roasted on an open fire and nothing was to be left of him. No bones were to be broken and the blood of the lamb was to be placed over the doorposts and side posts of the children of Israel's homes. When the death angel came into Egypt that fateful nigh and saw the blood, He would pass over the houses that were covered by the blood.

Now here is why the cross was necessary and here is something that you can shout about until you meet Jesus Christ face to face. The reason they chose a male lamb is because God would want a male lamb without blemish. They were told to roast the lamb for a particular reason. When roasting a lamb, a long splint is pressed down the lambs back and a short splint is pushed across His shoulders. The children of Israel thought that it was designed to help them turn the lamb while it was over the fire, but what they had was a lamb on a cross. Most importantly, the blood was used to cover the sins of the people and it led to their freedom from Egyptian bondage. Likewise, the blood of the Lamb sets us free from the bondage of the world and covers us completely. With this in mind, the blood of the lamb is our atonement.

Not only was the cross necessary because it was a fulfillment of prophecy foreshadowed, but it was also a fulfillment of a promise foretold. In Genesis 22, Abraham was severely tested. He was summoned by God to sacrifice his only son, Isaac. What made matters even worse, was God required that Abraham, Isaacs' father, be the responsible assailant for the crime. In faith, Abraham took Isaac and a few servants and spent three days looking for the right spot to kill

7: VICTORY through the CROSS OF CHRIST

his only son as a sacrifice to God. Finally, he located the place on one of the mountains in the region of Moriah.

While preparing to climb the mountain, Abraham told his servants at the base of the hill to remain with the donkeys because he and his son were going to worship and come right back. When Isaac and Abraham shared in conversation, Isaac said to his father, I have noticed that we have fire and we have plenty of wood *"...but where is the lamb..." (Gen. 22:7)*. To which Abraham responded, *"...God would provide Himself a lamb..." (Gen. 22:8).* A better translation of this verse would be, "God is going to become a lamb for us." To which you must ask yourself the question, when did that happen? It happened at the appointed time, when John saw Jesus Christ, who was Emmanuel, God with us, He called Him the Lamb of God who was present to take away the sins of the world (John 1:29). Where would this Lamb die? The answer is simple, at the cross!

Most importantly, the cross was necessary because it was the fulfillment of payment in full. If you are a Christian, you have been redeemed. There are four words used in the Greek New Testament that all mean to redeem and all of them apply to you as a believer in Jesus Christ. *Lutroo* means to redeem, but it means to buy a slave from the slave market. It means to pay a ransom. *Agoradzo* also translates into English as the word redeemed but it means to buy what you can afford to buy. *Exagoradzo* is very similar to the previous word and it means to buy something that is worthless. *Apollotrosis* translates redeemed but it means to purchase and pay the full price.

Are you rejoicing yet? If not, how can you hold your peace? All of these portraits of redemption apply to you! You were a slave to sin, but you have been redeemed. God decided to purchase you because He could afford to do it. You were a worthless, pitiful sinner but God looked at your trash and saw a treasure. He looked at your failures and saw a future. He did not purchase you from a discount store on a sale table. He paid full price for you. Where did He do that, you ask? By now you have to know the answer, at the cross!

Here is what the Bible says about the matter of your redemption:

> ***Christ hath redeemed us from the curse of the law, being made a curse for us: for it is written, Cursed is every one that hangeth on a tree: (Gal. 3:13)***
>
> ***Forasmuch as ye know that ye were not redeemed with corruptible things, as silver and gold, from your vain conversation received by tradition from your fathers; but with the precious blood of Christ,***

7: VICTORY through the CROSS OF CHRIST

as a lamb without blemish and without spot. (1 Pet. 1:18-19)

For there is one God and one mediator between God and men, the man Christ Jesus, who gave Himself a ransom for all, to be testified in due time. (1 Tim. 2:5-6)

In whom we have redemption through His blood, the forgiveness of sins, according to the riches of His grace. (Eph. 1:7)

What? Know ye not that your body is the temple of the Holy Ghost, which is in you, which ye have of God, and ye are not your own? For ye are bought with a price: therefore, glorify God in your body, and in your spirit, which are God's. (1 Cor. 6:19-20)

For he that is called in Lord, being a servant, is the Lord's freeman: likewise also he that is called, being free is Christ's servant. Ye are bought with a price: be not ye the servants of men. (1 Cor. 7:22-23)

The victory of redemption is best seen through the cross of Jesus Christ and in full knowledge of who He redeemed us from. In other words, if the cross is the place that the Lord redeemed us, who did He redeem us from? Please get this and hold on to this truth the rest of your life. Jesus had to rescue, ransom and redeem us from the hand of the enemy. Our adversary, the devil, held the deed to our destiny. To make matters worse, he would not let us go free. Satan had a firm grip on us and had no desire to let us go. But, Jesus died! Wait, He didn't just die, He suffered, bled, was beaten and He died! Through His redemptive death came our victory!

This is why the worship environment of any church should be a noisy place. Here is how the scriptures read regarding this matter, ***"Let the redeemed of the Lord say so, who He hath redeemed from the hand of the enemy: and gathered them out of the lands from the east and from the west, from the north and from the south….Oh, that men would praise the Lord for His goodness and for His wonderful works to the children of men" (Psalms 107:2,3,8 KJV).***

Several things happened on the cross the day Jesus Christ died for us that come along with redemption. With this in mind, at the moment Christ redeemed us He also justified us. This means that we were guilty in a court of law but we have been declared innocent by the presiding judge. Not only did He justify us; but He also sanctified us. This means that God

7: VICTORY through the CROSS OF CHRIST

has set us apart for His use and His glory. Most importantly, it means we have been glorified. This suggests that because we have been redeemed, we will forever live when we pass from time and ease into eternity.

The real shout of this chapter is found in the fact that beyond the cross is an empty tomb! Yes, He died, but the record says early Sunday morning He rose with all power in His hands! He is alive and the evidence of His life is He lives in every born-again believer of Jesus Christ!

Victory Happens Here

Victory through the cross of Christ means numerous things for the child of God. Here are just a few them:

1. I am God's child (St. John 1:12)
2. I am Christ's friend (St. John 15:15)
3. I have been justified (Romans 5:1)
4. I am united with the Lord (1 Cor.17)
5. I belong to God (1 Cor. 6:19-20)
6. I am a member of Christ's body (1 Cor. 6:19)
7. I am a saint and not a sinner (Eph. 1:1)
8. I have been adopted as God's child (Eph. 1:5)
9. I have access to God's throne (Eph. 2:18)
10. I am forgiven of all sins (Col. 1:14)

11. I am complete in Christ (Col. 2:10)
12. I am free from condemnation (Rom. 8:1-2)
13. I am assured of a great ending (Rom. 8:28)
14. I love God unconditionally (Rom. 8:35-39)
15. I am anointed by God (1 Cor. 1:21-22)
16. I am hidden with Christ in God (Col. 3:3)
17. I am confident that God will perfect me (Phil 1:6)
18. I am a citizen of heaven (Phil. 3:20)
19. I do not have to fear (2 Tim. 1:7)
20. I have grace to help (Heb. 4:16)
21. I am born of God (1 John 5:18)
22. I am the salt of the earth (Matt. 5:13-14)
23. I am a branch in God's vine (John 15:1-15)
24. I am chosen to bear fruit (John 15:16)
25. I am a personal witness for Christ (Acts 1:8)
26. I am God's sanctuary (1 Cor. 3:16)
27. I am a minister of reconciliation (2 Cor. 5:17-21)
28. I am God's co-worker (2 Cor. 6:1)
29. I am God's workmanship (Eph. 2:10)
30. I am VICTORIOUS (Phil. 4:13)

Chapter 8

VICTORY
in
SPIRITUAL WARFARE

Think About This

The times that we are currently living in are the last and evil days. Our culture has been infiltrated with darkness and we see it so much it has become common. Racism is not a demon of the past. It is still very much a demon of the present. Police shootings of unarmed men are commonplace. Marriages are failing by the thousands, children are disrespectful, men are marrying men, women are marrying women, husbands are creeping, wives are cheating and politicians are stealing, accepting kickbacks and taking bribes.

There are churches on every corner and yet no one can find the light. Poverty, famine, disease, world hunger is ever present. Systemic evil and technological invasion of personal privacy are happening every day of the week. It is so dark that people who are trying to live right seem like a ridiculous minority.

Suicide, homicide and genocide are household titles used by local media sources all of the time. Democracy is corrupt. Systems that were once trusted are no longer taken seriously and often questioned if not entirely discarded. Things are a mess right now. However, there is a remnant of faithful believers who will say to the world, I am for Christ and will fight for the faith until I die!

This is where real Christians find victory in the midst of spiritual warfare.

Let's Go Deeper

To understand where spiritual warfare began, we have to start with God. Before there was anything, there was God. In eternity past, God was one in essence and triune in personality, sovereign in power, superfluous in might, loving in His actions and omnipotent in His reign. God created angels and gave them one job assignment. They were to worship Him.

The most beautiful of all angels was Lucifer. He was called the son of the morning because he was so splendid to look upon. In fact, he was the angel of worship. On the day of his creation, God made beautiful color and robed Lucifer in it.

This was done so that when the glory of the Lord bounced off of Him, it would fill heaven with a rainbow. God also made music on the day of his birth. This was done so that when Lucifer opened his mouth it would sound like an orchestra. Everywhere God was, Lucifer went with Him, but something tragic happened. Lucifer caught a glimpse of himself and thought he should be worshiped and that is when all hell broke loose. God kicked Lucifer out of heaven and some of the angels that followed him were expelled as well. Here is how it reads in the scriptures,

How are you fallen from heaven O Lucifer, son of the morning! How are you cut down to the ground, you who weakened the nations. For thou hast said in thine heart, I will ascend into heaven, I will exalt my throne above the stars of God: I will also sit on the mount of the congregation on the farthest sides of the north: I will ascend above the heights of the clouds, I will be like the Most High. (Isaiah 14:12-14)

Do you get it yet? Lucifer was an angel. He was the guardian protector of the throne, but pride slipped in under his radar and made him think he should be worshipped as God. The Lord of heaven had to make it clear that the throne in glory was already occupied and it was His seat. With this in mind, God dismissed Lucifer from heaven. After being expulsed, Lucifer had to inhabit something, so he made earth and the territory surrounding it his new home. This is why Genesis 1:1 reads, ***"In the beginning God created the heavens and the earth."*** But, verse two reads ***"And the earth was without form and void and darkness was upon the face of the deep."***

Now ask yourself, what happened in verse two that made the earth void and without form, when it was fine in verse one? Here is the right answer. Verse one gives an account of the earth God created, but verse two gives you the details of what happened when Lucifer arrived. Everything became dark. Things became void. God has never made anything dark and void. But when Lucifer showed up, so did the darkness and it has been dark ever since.

Lucifer is our adversary. He is Satan. He is the old serpent. He is the accuser of the brethren. This is a legal term, which means that he plans to argue in court against God and you (Rev. 12:10). What is his argument? He contends that God is not just, gracious, loving or good. Satan's chief argument is to prove that God is unjust for throwing him out of heaven and confining him to earth and hell.

When God removed Lucifer, He did not promote another angel to take his place. Instead, God created another species. This creation would be called humankind. When God made

8: VICTORY in SPIRITUAL WARFARE

Adam, he was a masterpiece. This is why Lucifer hated him so badly. Adam took his place. This is why the serpent was already in the garden at creation and it is also why Satan wanted Adam to forsake God's instruction and fall.

In the Garden of Eden, God gave Adam everything he would ever need to be both totally satisfied and content. But, as we all know, Adam let us down and sinned. This was a great day for Satan in the courtroom of eternity. Satan thought he had won the battle for sure. It now looked hopeless for humanity because we would now all be trapped in sin with no way out. Satan apparently proved that God was unfair, unjust and not good because God gave Adam everything and he still sinned against Him. This kind of trickery was right up Satan's alley.

In the game of chess, Satan was about to yell, "checkmate!" But God said, "not so fast, I still have another move and it is going to blow you mind!" God's plan was so spectacular it would rattle Satan's mental cage and drop him to his knees forever. Here is the plan, ***"For God so loved the world that He gave His only begotten Son that whosoever believeth in Him should not perish, but have everlasting life" (John 3:16)!***

Since the first Adam blew it and sinned, God gave us a second Adam and the second Adam would be Himself in the person of His Son (1 Cor. 15:45)! Are you rejoicing yet? Stop waiting and get started! Yes, there is a spiritual battle going on but God is on our side, so we win!

Lucifer knows that he is a defeated foe. He knows that he will lose. However, misery loves company and he is doing everything in his power to deceive us. Satan is working diligently to make the generation we now live in an age that turns its back on God. It is why Satan created genocide during the time Mary was pregnant with Jesus. He wanted Jesus destroyed (Matt. 2). Satan even tried to kill Jesus at the cross. But he made one huge mistake, he lifted Jesus up for the world to see! For our Lord had already declared, **"And I, if I, be lifted up I will draw all men unto me" (John 12:32).**

Here is some even greater news, the battle is not actually ours it belongs to the Lord (2 Chronicles 20:14-22)! However, just because the Lord is fighting the battle does not mean you will escape without dealing with some demons of your own. With this in mind, it is imperative you know that demons are the unembodied spirits of fallen angels who were dismissed when Lucifer was cast out of heaven. They can attack people, places, and things.

When demons attack a believer, they normally follow the same pattern every time. They attack the mind. Once they alter the mind, they seek to dominate the body. Once they have dominion over a person's body, they seek to get that person to live contrary to the will of God.

8: VICTORY in SPIRITUAL WARFARE

Demons very seldom travel alone. They work in packs. The chief demon is the devil and his main objective is to kill, steal and destroy anything over which he gains control (John 10:10). Demons can cause sickness and dumbness (Luke 11:14), spiritual blindness (2 Cor. 4:3) and mental illness (Luke 9:42 and Mark 5:1-9). They cause believers to sin and miss the mark (John 13:2). They can cause true believers to live in a state of constant turmoil (Eph. 6:12). Demons cause murder (Gen. 4:8). They can even push people to commit suicide (Matt. 27:5). The bottom line here is that the devil and every one of his demons are the authors of confusion, chaos, darkness, and torment.

Never forget this, true believers are most susceptible to demonic attack when we are not in the word of God on a regular basis. God's Word feeds the spirit and empowers a believer to stand against temptation and demonic influences. When a Christian is away from the Word, we will always dwell in darkness. However, when we are in His Word we discover that the Psalmist was right. ***"Thy Word is a lamp unto my feet and a light unto my path" (Ps. 119:105).*** Here is a word of wisdom, when encountering a demonic attack stay in the Word of the Lord.

Secondly, believers can encounter demonic attack when we are in close association with other people who are struggling spiritually with demonic possession. Please remember this, demons can move from person to person. So be careful with whom you associate with at all times. If you are near a person who drinks, do not be shocked when you start trying alcoholic beverages. If you are near people who use drugs, do not be shocked when you start sampling dope.

The demons that your peers struggle with will soon become the demons that live in the den of your soul.

Lastly, Christians are susceptible to demonic influence when the flesh is out of control. Demons use our flesh against us, so never trust it. This is why the Apostle Paul admonished the churches of Galatia to "walk in the Spirit" (Gal. 5:16). This does not mean a believer should walk around in a trance of some sort. It simply means the child of God should be in constant fellowship with the Lord through the person of the Holy Spirit. In short, it means as a child of the King, the safest place for you during spiritual combat is near the throne of your Master.

Now here is the shout of this chapter. Even if you have been under demonic attack, it does not mean you have to stay there! Our God is a strong deliverer! God can take a gay man and restore his manhood. God can take a perverted woman and grace her with integrity. God can take an alcoholic and cause him to never touch another drink again. He can do it!

If you were to find your life as a Christian facing a demonic attack, James teaches us what should be done. Here is what the Bible says, ***"Submit yourselves therefore to God, resist the devil and he will flee from you" (James 4:7).*** In other words, get to the Lord and bow at His feet. Give your life back to Him because without Him you can do nothing. However, with God you can do all things. While you are in the presence of the Lord, who is your Father, rebuke the devil. To rebuke means to re-wound the enemy. When was he wounded the first time you ask? He was hit hardest at the cross where he was defeated. When the devil tries to remind you of your past, you remind him of his future.

Remember this, because Jesus Christ is on your side, your future has victory written all over it!

Victory Happens Here

The blessing of spiritual warfare as a believer in Jesus Christ is seen on the battlefield with saints that are dressed for warfare. Always get ready for battle and never approach spiritual combat unless you are ready for the occasion. Take a moment and read Ephesians 6:10-21. This is the longest chapter in the Bible on spiritual warfare and the believer. So read and get ready!

Most importantly, our victory in spiritual battle comes in one name. A name that we have been given permission to use for the purpose of casting out demons, tearing down strongholds and moving demonic influences. It is a name that is above every name (Phil. 2). It is a name that when mentioned demons in hell fear and tremble (James 2:19). It is a name that has within it healing power, strength, and deliverance. That name is Jesus Christ, Son of the living God (Mark 16:17, Mark 9:14-23, Matt. 17:14-20)!

Our victory in the spirit comes to us not because of our power, but because of His name!

Chapter 9

VICTORY
in
THE KINGDOM OF GOD

Think About This

At the moment you made the decision to give your life to Jesus Christ you became a citizen of another country. A land whose borders are from everlasting to everlasting and whose national flag is the blood stained banner of Jesus Christ. A people whose national language embraces every dialect known to human kind and whose army is a majestic myriad of angels that is set and ready for battle at a moment's notice. A culture whose political framework is not communism, socialism, or democracy, but a theocracy, governed by God for God. An economy whose socioeconomic infrastructure is built on a system of a commonwealth. A country whose citizenship contains immigration laws that embrace the "whosoever will" and whose national anthem is Amazing Grace.

At the moment you became a believer in Jesus Christ you gained residency into the greatest known country in the world. In your country, your leader is not elected or appointed, He reigns! He existed before was ever was and will continue until no more is no more. He is a sovereign ruler, whose decisions are immutable, whose blessings are undeniable and whose grace is unfathomable. In your country, the preamble and constitution are given to its citizens in a book called the Bible. In your homeland, foes are defeated and citizens are worshippers of its King.

In the country that you call home, the city has a master builder and its maker is God. The city sits in a perfect square. There are twelve gates to the city, with three gates being on each side of the building. Each gate bears the names of one of the Lord's disciples and each gate is seventy-five yards thick. Your eternal home has twelve foundations in it. Each foundation carries the name of one the twelve tribes of Israel. The streets of the place you call home are made of gold. However, it is not like any gold you have ever seen, for the gold of your city is transparent like glass.

In your homeland, the city is a perfect square and its length is equal to its height. The building is about fifteen hundred miles long and fifteen hundred miles high. One wall would

9: VICTORY in THE KINGDOM OF GOD

stretch from Houston and find its way to Los Angeles and will be some six hundred stories tall. In the country where you are from, there will be no need for sunlight or moonlight, for the glory of the Lord will light up the whole earth.

What is this Kingdom you ask? It is the Kingdom of our God and it is real. It will be the place where we live eternally with God to worship Him in spirit and in truth.

To be in God's Kingdom means that victory is a part of your lifestyle. For in His Kingdom, there is no defeat!

Let's Go Deeper

Jesus Christ came preaching the Kingdom. This was the core, crux, and center of everything He taught during His time on earth. In fact, the phrase "Kingdom of God" is mentioned four times in the Gospel of Matthew, fourteen times in Mark, thirty-two times in Luke and twice in John. If you were to include the phrase "Kingdom of Heaven" in this list, Jesus would have mentioned the Kingdom another twenty-two times while teaching, telling stories and healing during His sojourn amongst us. In short, Jesus wanted those near Him to know that the Kingdom was at hand.

A kingdom is best defined as a place where a king rules, reigns, remains and has regency. Kings are never elected. In other words, kingdoms are not democracies. The term democracy is derived from a Latin word which means to be governed by the people. So in a democratic government, like the one that we live in right now, we have a right to elect our leaders. If the leaders we elect serve well, we re-reelect them. If they serve poorly, we have a right to vote them out and vote new people into office. This is not how a kingdom works. A king becomes king because of family lineage. The heir to the throne is born into royalty and becomes king because he has been blessed with the royal right to reign.

In the Kingdom of God, the Lord of creation is our King. In fact, He is not just our King, but He is the King of kings! There has been no other ruler to compare to Him, nor will there ever be. Our King is in a class all by Himself.

The only way into the Kingdom of God is to be born again. This is the message Jesus shared with Nicodemus, the ruler of Jews. One night Nicodemus came to Jesus because he knew Jesus had a connection with God the Father like no one else had. Nicodemus had never seen miracles like the ones Jesus had produced. While talking with Jesus, the Lord tells this Jewish leader how to enter the kingdom that He leads. Jesus says to him, ***"...except a man be born again, he cannot see the kingdom of God" (John 3:3b, KJV).***

This statement was very perplexing to this very intelligent Jewish man. Nicodemus asks, "how am I supposed to do that now that I am already out of my mother's womb?" (paraphrase). Jesus takes a moment to teach him by saying,

9: VICTORY in THE KINGDOM OF GOD

"that which is born of flesh is flesh and that which is born of the Spirit is spirit" (John 6:6, KJV). In other words, "Nicodemus, you have been born of the flesh but the Kingdom I lead is one rooted and grounded in the spirit and requires a spiritual rebirth if you are going to enter it" (Paraphrase).

A huge question mark now appears on the face of Nicodemus and Jesus eases his thoughts, soothes his mind and shows him what this whole thing is all about. He says, ***"…..whosoever believeth in Him should not perish but have eternal life. For God so loved the world that He gave His only begotten Son, that whosoever believeth in Him should not perish, but have everlasting life" (John 3:15b-16, KJV).***

Now here is what is deep. In connection with His Kingdom talk, Jesus told people to repent (Luke 13:5). The term repent comes from two Greek words that are very closely related in pronunciation but very different in meaning. One word is the term *metamelomai*. The prefix *meta* means after and *melomai* is where we borrow our word melancholy from, which means to feel sad. Therefore, repent in one instance means that after you sin, you should feel bad or sad. A believer should never sin before God knowingly and not feel anything. A feeling of sadness should follow. But, sadness for sin does not qualify a person to be a citizen of the kingdom.

There is another term used for the word repent in the Greek and it is *metanoeo*. Of course, *meta* means after, but *noeo* means the change. When both words are put together, repentance means after the change. Now here is the question that should be running through your mind right about now, what change? The change Jesus is speaking of was both personal and political. It took place whenever a person decided they wanted to change kings and kingdoms. That individual would repent. They would change their mind about one king and the kingdom that King represented for a new king and his kingdom.

In a real sense, repentance is spiritual immigration reform. It takes place whenever people leave one king for a new one. It is a conscious decision made on behalf of the individual that I do not want my old king; I need, want and desire my new king.

This is what happens every time a person comes to Christ. They are saying in a real sense I am through with my old king. Today I am changing kings and kingdoms. I want to leave the kingdom of darkness for the kingdom of light. I want to depart from the kingdom of my past to the kingdom of my future. I want King Jesus to be my King!

Like any other government, the Kingdom of God has laws that govern it and its citizens. Keep in mind, the laws in a kingdom come from the lips of the King. These laws are

9: VICTORY in THE KINGDOM OF GOD

called decrees. Kings make decrees and once a declaration from a king is made, the thing he has decreed becomes the law. With this in mind, four laws serve as foundational pillars in the Kingdom of God.

The Law of Reciprocity (Matthew 13:8)

The law of sowing and reaping is very powerful. In short, it says that what you sow, you will also reap. The blessing of this law is once you sow, what you reap is always more, much more. If you sow watermelon seeds, you do not only reap more seeds you reap watermelons! This law prevails throughout the entire kingdom. It has at its core the blessing of giving that makes living more meaningful. The curse of this law is that if you sow nothing, you reap nothing.

This is why all Christians should tithe. The word tithe means tenth and as a believer in the Lord Jesus Christ, a tenth of your income should be sown back into the kingdom so it lacks no economic shortage on earth. Politically the tithe is a tax. However, unlike taxes in America, kingdom tithes are not obligatory, they are voluntary. In short, you do not pay tithes like you pay taxes. You give tithes because no debt is owed. Here is how it works. Consider the blessings of our King. Consider how wonderful He has been, how kind, sweet, merciful, gracious and loving He has been. Now ask yourself this question, "Is my King worth a dime to me?" If your easy answer was yes, sow the tithe into the Kingdom.

If you made a deposit of $1,000.00 last month, your tithe to the Kingdom is $100.00. If you made $3,000.00 last week, your tithe to the Kingdom is $300.00. It is just that simple.

Now here is a moment where real rejoicing should be released. Our Kingdom is a Commonwealth. This is why Jesus Christ made the statement at the onset of His ministry that He had the Gospel for the poor (Luke 4:18). We think good news for a poor person would be money in their hand. However, Jesus did not come to give poor people a check. He came to give poor people a new government. Are you shouting yet? This is exciting Kingdom news! In our Kingdom, poverty cannot exist. The reason why there can be no poverty is because in a commonwealth, the wealth is common. You see, in a Kingdom, the citizens are connected to the wealth of the King and our King is rich. He is so rich that He holds the deed of imminent domain to the earth. Yes, Jesus said that, *"...the poor you will have with you always" (Mark 14:7)*; however, the reason for this statement was because Jesus knew there would always be people who reject His throne. To accept Him as King says "my poverty is over because my King is going to take care of me!"

Keep this in mind, our King has never asked you to give Him what you do not have. In fact, the opposite is true. The

9: VICTORY in THE KINGDOM OF GOD

King wants you to give it because He knows you have it. How does He know you have it? He gave it to you. Everything you have came from the King.

When you take what the King has given to you and sow it into the fertile ground of the Kingdom, it will return to you every time.

The Law of Use (Matthew 25:14-30)

The law of use simply says use or lose what God has blessed you with. This law is life changing and here is why. All citizens of the Kingdom receive gifts and blessings from the King. However, what you choose to do with those gifts and blessings are entirely up to the recipient. When you use what the King has given you, He blesses it. He increases it. He favors it. He graces it and causes it to prosper. However, if you choose not to use it, the same King who gave it to you will take it away.

Keep this in mind, the reason most people do not use the gifts the King has given them is because they are too busy comparing their gifts to the gifts of others. So instead of using their gift, they put their God-given gifts down because it is not like someone else's gift. This offends our King.

Hear this people of the Kingdom of God; use what you have been given to the Glory of our God. It does not matter how small your gift is, use it for His glory. It does not matter what you think about your gift or even what people say about your gift, use your gift for His Glory and He will bless your gift like crazy.

The Law of Love (John 13:34)

The law of love is our Kingdom's trademark and authenticator. The only way to know for sure a person is a citizen of our country is to measure the love they have for God and other people. This is provocative because we do not have a problem loving God. Most Christians are quick to say without any hesitation they love God. However, the problem comes in when we are challenged to love each other. Love in our Kingdom is a law. Therefore, to not love, makes you a law breaker.

Please know, love in the Kingdom is not some warm fuzzy feeling. Love is a decision we make to treat others like we would want to be treated and to be a visible, virtual manifestation of God's presence where ever we go. That is love.

Unfortunately, most of what we see in the Kingdom is legalism and not love. Legalism occurs when we like people who are like us. It takes place when people come near us who fit into our little concentric circle of contact. Legalism is best seen when we make a list of rules and get individuals who are like us to comply with them. However, the same list is used to

9: VICTORY in THE KINGDOM OF GOD

keep people who are not like us out. Keep this in mind, legalism is nothing more than hatred hiding behind a cross. It is far from God and has nothing to do with our King.

Love is seen in the Kingdom when people who are not like us and do not fit into our circles come near and we accept them as God accepts us. That is love! Love allows adulterers to find mercy in God's presence (John 8). Love makes room for a demon possessed crazy man to be used by God in his hometown for the Kingdom's sake (Mark 5). Love makes room for tax collectors and harlots to join you for dinner (Mark 2:15). Love makes room for hypocrites, like Peter, to be lead disciples (Mark 14). Love embraces a woman who has had five husbands and is living with one that is not quite hers at present (John 4). Love hates religious people who feel superior to others (Luke 18:11). Love is God for God is love (1 John 4:8).

To know God is to know love! Love is powerful. If you slap love, it hugs you. If you wound love, it restores you. If you hate to love, love loves you. If you betray love, it forgives you. If you drop love, it picks you up. If you forsake love, it embraces you. If you fail to love, it never fails you. If you nail love to a cross, it cries "Father forgive them for they know not what they do." If you stab love on the side, it will say, "today thou shalt be with me in paradise." If you hurt love, it will pardon you. If you kill love, it rises again. If you bury love, you should anticipate a resurrection.

Love is what our Kingdom is all about. This is why you should actuate love, accentuate love, appreciate love, articulate love, accelerate love, accommodate love, activate love, adjudicate love, advocate love, allocate love, anticipate love, culminate love, captivate love, celebrate love, commemorate love, communicate love, commentate love, cultivate love, corroborate love, concentrate love, consolidate love, consummate love, coordinate love, create love, delegate love, delineate love, demonstrate love, diplomate love, domesticate love, donate love, duplicate love, elevate love, emancipate love, emanate love, emulate love, enumerate love, exaggerate love, exasperate love, illuminate love, inaugurate love, imitate love, immediate love, impersonate love, inflate love, initiate love, innovate love, innumerate love, mandate love, obligate love, propitiate love, punctuate love, rejuvenate love, radiate love, reactivate love, recultivate love, reiterate love and relate love! Love! To love our King is to love, Love. Love is what wins and love is what the Kingdom and the King are all about.

Take a moment and read 1 Corinthians 13. Love is what makes the difference every time. This is why we should be people of love because love is the fruit of our victory.

9: VICTORY in THE KINGDOM OF GOD

The Law of Forgiveness (Matthew 18:21)

This law says let them go. That is it. It is just that simple. No if's, and's or doubts about it. Most importantly, forgiveness is best defined as our ability to release the people who have caused us pain and to remember what caused the pain, without hurting anymore from the pain that it caused.

Forgiveness comes from a Greek word that paints three pictures for you to consider. Forgiveness paints the picture of a boat whose anchor has been released from a rock beneath the surface of the vessel. When the anchor is lifted, the boat is no longer bound and is free to move with the wind and the current because the boat's bondage is over.

Forgiveness is like a prisoner who has been locked up for years and years. But, has now been released from jail and can now go free.

Forgiveness is the picture of a divorce. At one time, both parties were bound by a covenant, but a bill of divorce has been granted and the two part and go their separate ways.

In all three portraits, the resolve is the same; that which is bound goes free. The Kingdom of God is not a Kingdom of bondage, but a Kingdom of freedom. You cannot serve the King bound. Freedom is a must for service to the King. Therefore, forgiveness, no matter how difficult it may be, is a must for those who are citizens of our Kingdom.

It is imperative to note that forgiveness is reciprocal. The only way to receive it from the King is to give it to others who you know do not deserve it.

Victory Happens Here

Jesus Christ often taught in large crowds. During His time of teaching to large groups, He often told parables. A parable is a kingdom story connected to a kingdom principle that keeps the Kingdom hidden from those who are not a part of it. In other words, parables were used to prohibit espionage from taking place. However, it is apparent from the teachings of our King that His Kingdom is both present and coming simultaneously. In short, the Kingdom of our God is both right now and not yet. In other words, it is here already. We know that because the Kingdom of God lives in the hearts of every citizen of our country that loves the King!

There is much more still yet to come! In the not too distant future, the Kingdom of our God will reign on earth and heaven will consume the earth. Until that day comes, live victoriously like subjects on earth who belong to the Kingdom of God, which is in heaven!

Chapter 10

VICTORY
through
THE SECOND COMING OF CHRIST

Think About This

Without a shadow of a doubt, we know that Jesus Christ came to earth some two thousand years ago. We know this to be true because the annals of human history speak clearly concerning His existence. Moreover, the Bible tells us the story of His coming as no other book does. Matthew says that at the birth of Jesus, the cosmological structure of the starry skies took on some different attributes because one star lit up the sky. He also says that heaven's angels were so excited they shouted, ***"Glory to God in the highest! Peace on earth, goodwill towards men."*** Matthew say the Magi (wise men) had apparently watched for the King's arrival for quite some time and when they spotted the star, they picked up gifts of gold, frankincense, and myrrh and left all of their treasures behind to find the child who would be born King of the Jews.

Matthew further contends when the wise men did find Jesus, they worshiped Him and presented their gifts to Him because He was the Messiah. He was the Anointed One. He was the Christ child. He was the one sent from heaven to save His people from their sin. He was the one who would be the perfect sacrifice, the sacrificial Lamb. He would be the one who would reveal God's love to us in such a way that it would change the course of human history forever.

History is clear, Jesus has been to earth because the record reflects the fact that blinded eyes were opened, wounded hearts were healed, water was turned into wine, a withered hand was made straight, lepers were cleansed, Peter walked on water, a demoniac was delivered, a person with paralysis was restored and a dead man named Lazarus was resurrected.

Even though Jesus has been to earth before, the Bible teaches us He had to leave so that the Comforter would come. Scripture also clearly states after the resurrection, Jesus was seen by as many as five hundred people at one time (1 Cor. 15). Most importantly, Jesus told His disciples to stay in Jerusalem until the Holy Ghost came and while He spoke to them a cloud received Him into heaven (Acts 1:1-8).

10: VICTORY through THE SECOND COMING OF CHRIST

Now here is what is so exciting. While Jesus was being received into heaven, two angels stood by and delivered a soul-stirring word to them that would change everything. They said, ***"…Ye men of Galilee, why stand ye gazing up into heaven? This same Jesus, which is taken up into heaven, shall so come in like manner as ye have seen Him go into heaven" (Acts 1:11).***

The second coming of Jesus Christ will be the most awesome day the world has ever seen. Believers all over the globe, Protestants, Catholics, Apostolics, Church of Christ, Church of God in Christ, Assemblies of God and all of those who love Jesus, will be caught up to meet Him in the air. Those who are left behind will be in a state of disbelief, while others will contend that aliens have invaded the planet. However, it will not be aliens who take persons from this sinful earth. It will be the call of a loving, caring omnipotent God saying, "I have come like a thief in the night just like I told you I would!"

When Jesus returns, planes that have believers for pilots will crash. Taxicabs with believers for drivers will instantly wreck. Boats with believers at the helm will be abandoned. Chemical plants and big industries will find themselves without numerous employees and the church will learn who the true believers are because it will be harvest time. It will be a time to separate the wheat from the tare.

It will spell victory for all believers the world over!

Let's Go Deeper

The second coming of Christ is going to happen and we have proof regarding this truthful fact. First of all, Jesus declared it, *"In my Father's house are many mansions, if it were not so I would have told you. I go to prepare a place for you and if I go and prepare a place for you I will come again and receive unto you unto myself; that where I am, there ye may be also" (John 14:2-3).*

We also have the testimony of the Lord's Supper. In this rite, our communion table is both a sign and symbol. It is a sign in that it points to an end that is yet future. It is also a symbol because it helps us participate in our victorious celebration while we are still here on earth. Here is what the Bible says, *"For as often as ye eat this bread, and drink this cup, ye do show the Lord's death till He comes" (1 Cor. 11:26)*

We even have the testimony of heavenly beings that Jesus is going to return (Acts 1:10-11). Moreover, the Apostle Paul preached it (Titus 2:13, 2 Cor. 15:51-58), John the last living Apostle declared it when he said, *"Behold He (Jesus) cometh with the clouds and every eye shall see Him, and they which pierced Him; and all kindred's of the earth shall wail because of Him (Rev. 1:7).*

10: VICTORY through THE SECOND COMING OF CHRIST

Most importantly, Matthew put it on this wise, ***"Watch, therefore; for ye know not what hour your Lord doth come. But know this, that if the goodman of the house had known in what watch the thief would come, he would have watched and would not have suffered his house to be broken up. Therefore be ye also ready, for in such an hour as ye think not, the Son of man cometh" (Matt. 24:42-44).***

We are confident that the Lord is going to come back and just like millions missed His first coming, even more will miss His second coming. This will be the case because most people do not understand the manner and method of His return.

With this in mind, please know that the second coming of Jesus Christ will happen in two stages. The Rapture and the Revelation. Let us briefly examine both.

The Rapture

The term rapture is not found anywhere in the scripture. It is used in the Latin Vulgate Translation of the Bible. The word used for rapture in the Vulgate was *raptizo*. We borrow it to make our word rapture. It means immediately. It means at the blink of an eye. Therefore, we can conclude that the rapture will happen quickly.

Here are some solid rapture facts and truths to hold on to:

1. The rapture will be for those saints who have died in Christ and are waiting for His return.
2. It will also be for believers who are still alive and remain when He comes back.
3. It will be a total surprise.
4. Jesus will not be seen in His glory. He will come as a thief.
5. As a thief, He will leave much more than He takes.
6. Jesus will have an entry and an exit strategy.
7. Jesus will not notify anyone that He is coming.
8. He will not come to stay or establish a throne on earth.
9. The reason Jesus came the first time was to set the stage for His coming a second. A good thief never breaks into a place He has never been before.
10. It will take place in the air.

The Apostle Paul describes this moment so beautifully when he says,

Behold I show you a mystery, we shall not all sleep, but we shall all be changed. In a moment, in the twinkling of an eye, at the last trump: for the trumpet shall sound, and the dead shall be raised

10: VICTORY through THE SECOND COMING OF CHRIST

incorruptible, and we shall be changed. For this corruptible must put on incorruption, and this mortal shall have put on immortality, then shall be brought to pass the saying that is written, Death is swallowed up in victory. O death, where is thy sting? O grave, where is thy victory? The sting of death is sin and the strength of sin is the law. But thanks be to God, which giveth us the victory through our Lord Jesus Christ. Therefore, my beloved brethren, be ye steadfast, unmoveable, always abounding in the work of the Lord, forasmuch as ye know that your labor is not in vain in the Lord. (1 Cor. 15:51-58)

The Revelation

The revelation will differ from the rapture in many ways. It will be majestic and life changing. Here are some revelation facts to consider:

1. Christ will appear and everyone will see Him.
2. He will appear in His Glory!
3. It will take place on earth.
4. The purpose will be to establish an eternal reign and a Kingdom that will never end.
5. It will take place a few years after the rapture.

6. When it happens, it too will be a surprise.
7. Believers will be with Him arrayed in fine white linen. He will appear as the Lion of the Tribe of Judah

Here is what the Apostle John wrote regarding this matter,

And I saw heaven opened, and behold a white horse; and he that sat upon him was called Faithful and True, and in righteousness He doth judge and make war. His eyes were as a flame of fire, and on His head were many crowns; and He has a name written, that no man knew, but He Himself. And He was clothed with a vesture dipped in blood: and His name was called the Word of God. And the armies which were in heaven followed Him upon white horses, clothed in fine white linen, white and clean. And out of His mouth goeth a sharp sword, that with it He should smite the nations: and He shall rule them with a rod of iron: and He treadeth the winepress and wrath of Almighty God. And He hath on His vesture and on His thigh a name written, King of Kings and Lord of Lords. (Rev. 19:11-16)

This is why believers the world over should live in victory because, in the end, we win!

Conclusion

To say that you are victorious is one thing, but to say that you are victory is another. People who are victorious win some and lose some. In your case, things are different and the difference for you is God. You do not win some and lose some, like most people, you win them all. Of course, you will have ups and downs. Certainly, you will have good days and challenging moments. However, you are so prone to victory until even when you lose, you still win.

Every part of this book has spelled it out for you and what you believe about the Lord has, by faith, will without a doubt, come to fruition. Victory describes the essence of who you are in Christ and victory gives details to what you will possess when time is no more. Get used to it. Wear it like it has been tailor made for you. Walk in it. Worship in it. Live like you have it! More importantly, become it! Victory! Victory! Victory!

It describes what and who you are in Jesus Christ!

John R. Adolph

Other Books and Articles by Dr. John R. Adolph

Books:
I'm Changing the Game
Not Without A Fight
I'm Coming Out of This
Just Stick to the Script
Victorious Christian Living Volume I
Victorious Christian Living Volume II
Let Me Encourage You Volume I
Let Me Encourage You Volume II
The Him Book
Marriage Is For Losers
Celibacy is for Fools
Better Together
Based On A True Story
Back To The Table
Help Me Handle This

Articles-Zondervan Press
He Loves Me, I'm Certain That He Loves Me
His Love Made The Difference
God's Mind Is Made Up; He Loves You

For more information contact:
Dr. John R. Adolph
C/O Advantage Books
info@advbooks.com

To order additional copies of this book or other books by Pastor Adolph visit advbookstore.com

Saint Johns, FL
we bring dreams to life

www.ingramcontent.com/pod-product-compliance
Lightning Source LLC
Chambersburg PA
CBHW071152090426
42736CB00012B/2308